# Earn Money From Home
# *10 Ways To Double Your Salary*

by
Winston J. Duncan

# Table of Contents

# Introduction

Many people dread getting out of their comfort zones, I was one of them. I could never imagine my life without a steady pay-check, even though that meant working for someone I simply loathed, doing the same thing for years until I reached a breaking point. Thankfully, with the motivation from my friends and family, I dared to step out from my comfort zone of being in a secured job and looked at the option of working from home and setting up my business to fulfill my dreams.

I am a mother for two beautiful children, and never wanted to leave home after I got married even though I had to work; since we needed the money. It was hard to manage the house and job, since my job demanded extensive travelling, as I was into sales.

I used to look at people who were successful entrepreneurs and wonder - how do they do it? The answer to that unfolds a combination of consistent hard work and persistent determination. There are no free lunches in this world, one has to go out there, do what they believe in, and get what it takes to be an achiever.

This is something I realized when I was trying to seek answers to some of the questions I asked myself. Thanks to me asking those questions, I now have successfully quit the job, which I loathed and set up my own business. I now get to spend more than enough time with my girls, pay attention to the house, and I am proud that I have made a name for myself doing what I love to do the most.

In this book, I am going to share with you some simple tips on being self employed, separating the do's from the don'ts and 10 different ways to double your salary. Of course the salary or income may not exactly restrict itself to get doubled; it can multiply by many folds.

If you find your niche among these and are willing to take the plunge, my only suggestion to you is this – **Go for It!**

*"If you don't build your dream someone will hire you to help build theirs"* –

*Tony Gaskins*

# Chapter 1:
# Pros of Working from Home

Let us start with the good news first. Here are the some of the pros of being your own boss and starting your own business.

## You can be anywhere and still be a Business owner

Where you are based, does not matter. Thanks to the internet, the whole world is your playground. You have access to clients just about anywhere in the world, as long as they have an internet connection. If you ardently put your efforts into setting up your business from home, you can easily go global with minimum expense.

You can work from a remote town or life in a city, work prospects will be available as long as you market yourself well. Another good thing is you can take a vacation when you want and still be able to respond to clients from your phone or laptop in case of an emergency.

## Time Spent Well

When you work at an organization, there are usually many constraints. You have a tight schedule to follow, a fixed time to reach work, and probably stay until the end or beyond your working hours many a times, whether you want it or not.

Most people get exhausted in the drudgery of work life. Some work in a rotating shift and the schedule takes a toll on their physical and mental health. Many do not get enough sleep and have to rush out early in the morning to make sure they are not late for work. Then there is the droning routine of incessantly working with just a couple of breaks in between. Not only is this routine tiring but it is very stressful too.

With a home business, it is all about being your own boss, following work hours according to your choice and feasibility. You can do what you want, when you want; as long as you don't deviate from your goal! The flexibility that working from home or being your own boss offers is unmatched to that of a regular job.

**Anyone Can Do It!**

It should not matter what age, race, gender, you are. Absolutely anyone can start to earn money from home. If you are someone fed up of your boring and exhausting job, but cannot quit yet, you could always begin by using your free time to start up a business from home to earn extra money. Just think of a suitable venture and set it up online! To be frank, there is no dearth of what you can start up (I have discussed that in detail in Chapter 4)

**Set a Business on a Minimal Budget**

No matter where you work from, while you are starting out, you require a workspace. Hit upon any nook and corner in your house that would work for you. The essential requirements are a phone, a first-rate computer, internet, printer, fax machine etc. These are some bare minimum investments that will work a long way for you.

You don't need a state of the art office space, a sexy assistant or a fancy coffee machine. One small corner in your house and the basic equipments to get started can make you the CEO of your business. If your business does not necessitate storage then these utilities are enough. However, if you plan to sell products and have to dispatch them, you require a space to store them in the mean time. (In my opinion, to begin with, the garage comes in handy)

## No Capping on Income!

With an established home business, you no longer have to wait for the paycheck at the beginning of the month. Your income now depends entirely on you and there is no salary cap to it. It is all about how well you do in your business, which is directly aligned to your earning potential. Trust me when I say this, the world is your oyster if you are driven enough to make it happen.

## Additional Savings

When you work from home, you don't have to wear a suit or tie, cake your face with makeup to look presentable and invest in expensive shoes. Yes, this is one expense we somehow don't calculate when we spend hundreds of dollars for our upkeep, so that we look presentable to run someone else's business.

Image the amount of money you will save on gas since you don't have to drive to work. Not to forget precious time that you will save since you don't have to brave the peak hour traffic.

Well, to be honest, these are just some of the many pros of working from home.

# Chapter 2:
# The Legislations about Working from Home

In the last edition of this book we had a thorough discussion on the type of work which is labeled as "working from home". That edition gave us a tremendous feedback and based on queries of our prestigious writers, we felt the need about writing this second edition of our book.

Greatly admired by the idea employment by following work from home, many of the readers are interested in knowing the legislative position of this field of work. They were interested in knowing that if all the perquisites of this particular type of employment are protected under the employment law and other corporate laws. Here is a brief writing to make our readers aware about the legislative notions of this career.

## Define your particular position:

The industry, which deals with all those who work from home, is a widespread area. This industry is gaining momentum day by day, so it is also added to a number of actors and agents. The type of legislation and a particular act pertaining to your work needs a careful pointing of your particular position. Whatever you do at home as your career, you may fall into one of the following major categories:

## Self-employed:

If you work solely at your own, you are categorized as self-employed. The self-employed workers interact with the clients directly and no other agency or third party is involved. Whether you work on a multidimensional scale, or smaller limited scale, being self-employed you interact with the client directly and all payments and project submission is carried out between you and your client.

## Limited company contractor:

If you work from home, but you provide the services by dealing as a company, you may fall in the category of limited company contractor. In this case the individual who works from home undergoes various contracts and business agreements with the client so that whenever a project is handed over all the agreements and business transactions are undergone under the name of the company. The further details may include the contractual agreements and the type of various other agreements signed by the person, as a private limited contractor. There are many instances when people work from home using their family business name but when it comes to agreement details, they use their own name. Both these conditions must be taken seriously, as the legislation status is different in both cases.

## The umbrella workers:

You can get engaged with a company and still work from home. The umbrella companies can provide you the overreaching employment contract. Although there is no any kind of ownership as a worker yet it is a safe mode to enjoy working from home and keeping away from the panic of running your own company. It is a kind of linkage between your client and you. Instead of getting all the time spent in finding the clients and then making the transaction, you directly hand over your project to the umbrella company.

## The status Of working from home varies

When you are considering the legal status of working from your home, it is essential that you may have a clear depiction of your particular position of your work status, as described above. Based on these variable positions the different categories of work laws include the following section of legislations pertaining to work from home.

## The minimum wage

This part of legislation is particularly important when you are working under the umbrella company or working through a third party contractor. The law permits the workers who are employed at home that they can ask for the minimum wage level which is announced by the government.

Being working from home under the umbrella will disburse a wage to the worker plus the additional expenditure. However the income tax will be deducted under the PAYE scheme (Pay as You Earn)

The umbrella company will maintain a pre mentioned fee, which can be adjusted either weekly or monthly. Most of the time this fee is not deducted for the time spans when the worker is not on an assignment or when there is a time laps between two consecutive assignments. The company may also be in an agreement to deduct a lump sum amount later to be given to the worker, like the holiday allowances or insurance deductions.

The umbrella company is protected under the law to deduct all kinds of amounts like previously mentioned taxes, insurances additives and other allowances form workers gross sums. In the legislation, it is allowed as the umbrella company relies on this source as a source of income, so they are given this option that they make a mutual consent with the workers to make these deductions.

## Health and security

There are a number of acts and law policies prevalent in different parts of the world, which ask for a sustainable protection of workers' health and security. These policies also cover the workers who are working from home.

If there is a worker who works from home under a self-employed status, he is self-responsible for all the security concerns, particularly if the work assignments involve handling or use of any dangerous equipment or material.

In case of the umbrella companies or third party contractors it is the responsibility of the company to provide the thorough training and the necessary monitoring for making it sure that the health and security standards are met by the worker at home.

In case of any special arrangements needed for the endurance of health and safety protection, the employing company cannot charge anything from the worker, in lieu of health and security arrangements. Under the laws and acts this is the sole responsibility of the third party contractors or Umbrella Company. To make it sure all the workers employed, whether at real office or at home are given proper safety and health protection shield.

## Fake job offers

In the last edition of this book we have provided our readers with a number of different options that can be entailed for pursuing a career form home. It covered a large area of services, which involved both technical and nontechnical work. But all over the world, there have been instances where the individuals working from home, whether as self-employed or as workers in Umbrella Company, were caught by fraudulent agents. It caused them not only the monetary losses, but also the mental and emotion de-motivation for pursuing it as a career. So a number of state agencies have formed law acts to save these individuals from different kind of losses.

If you are a self-employed worker then all you can do is to file the case within the workers' law court, so that the proper investigations can be made to reveal all the suspected who were involved in the fake job offer. The law also provides a proper guideline for all the self-employed workers at home to ensure the credibility of the client for whom they will be working and providing their services.

In case you are pursuing as a home worker under an umbrella company or any other contractors, you are usually at a safe position as the employer in this case will be the contracting company and they are charging a proper fee from the worker, for this service. They are bound to ensure the eradication of any fraudulent or fake job offer. The worker can also go in the court if any misdeed or fraud occurs on the behalf of the recruiting company. In this regard the formulation and the signing of all types of written document play a significant part to provide a secure and loss free position to the worker.

**Other legal issues to be taken care of:**

It is the responsibility of both the worker and the recruiting company, if any, to make sure that the project or task designated to be performed at home is suitable to be performed in the premises of the home. You cannot pursue any work at home that may cause any environmental or social damage to the surrounding community.

Moreover, if there is any kind of equipment needed for the project or the activity, it must not be hazardous to the community as well as the worker.

All the legal issues considered above, play a critical role if you are interested in making a firm and continuous career by working from home.

# Chapter 3:
# The career orientation of working from home

In the previous discussion we have largely talked about the extent of dependency of human life at work. We have highlighted that how the human existence is dependent upon the proper selection of work. Earning a living is no doubt a challenge that is why people find it difficult to get the most accurate form of working. Basically, this book is a guide to all those who want to earn a living through working at their homes.

But when we talk about this aspect of working with a number of questions are put forward. Many of the people ask that is it a proper career? But we have to tell you that this aspect of working as gone so far that it has taken the form of a whole career, where people are earning an attractive earning through this working dimension.

## Career means earning

If we start the different aspects of career both within the home and outside, we can find a number of similarities. One such similar aspect is the ability of both to allow the individual to earn a living for one's self. So if you are working from home, you can easily get a good amount of earnings. Based on different types of tasks done at home, the amount of earning may vary; however, working from home is not for free. You can charge anything depending upon the extent of efforts. If you are really good at your skills, the chances are bright that you can get a handsome amount of money, while enjoying your work from home. So working from home satisfies one aspect of a work being a career, which is capable of providing an earning.

## Career means opportunities

Now moving towards the broader aspects of a career we can see that all those careers in the field of working are considered respectful and bright, for which there is a huge market. It is because the wider array of opportunities always makes a job or career more worthwhile and attractive. If we examine our subject of interest from this perspective, we can see that the field of working from home is full of opportunities. From our last edition of the book you can easily view these innumerable opportunities, where the field of working from home has become so diverse. You can choose anything depending upon your particular skill sets and capabilities. So working from home is surely a career because it encompasses a number of opportunities for all those who are interested in it. If you consider a career as full of opportunities, then working from home can have your way both as a worker and as an entrepreneur

## Career denotes utilization of skills

Based on another dimension, we can discuss that what a career provides to the skills of an individual?? For all those careers which are renowned in the world one thing is more common, all these careers make perfect utilization skills of the candidate who is holding a particular position. All the hiring and recruitment is done through analyzing the skills which are most appropriate for a particular task. Based on all these realities, what is the purpose of doing work from home? Surely all this work will be demanding a particular skill set which will allow the individual to complete the task. So this career is also fully utilizes the skills of the individual. We should not think that if someone is working from home, he is capable of doing nothing that is why he has chosen this career. In reality, like all other careers working from home makes best use of one's skills and competencies.

## Career entails polishing of skills

When in a career the recruitment and hiring is done on the basis of the availability of a particular type of competencies, then it is believed that the candidate will use these skills. Once the individual starts working on the position, he gets periodic and frequent chances to use these skills, so that continues polishing of these skills occurs. Now what about working from home? No matter what task have you taken or what type of projects you work upon, you surely on some competencies and set of knowledge. Based on these skills you get the task and you fulfill it. It is a periodic cycle where using the skills overran and over again will result in the polishing of skills. One gets more refined in his skills. It is the basic notion for all types of careers. If we examine the same cycle of utilization and polishing of skills we can easily label the working from home as a career.

## Career makes you cherish a better living:

If we start discussing the purpose of making a pursuable career, we will come to a number of variable realties. Everyone wants to have a better living without any financial hurdles and jumps; one always wants to choose a better opportunity to work as a career has long lasting effects on one's life. Working from home entails the same potentials and can lead your path towards a remarkable life style and extraordinary living. In the subsequent sections we will guide you to make working from home, practical and result oriented. It is a career which has full potential to grant you an outstanding life style. So we have to consider it a proper career, which possesses all the basic features of a formalized way of working.

In the above discussion we have made an elaborated discussion to convince our readers that working from home is no less than a career. If you are pursuing it you are surely following a career.

# Chapter 4:
# Do Your Home Work

Don't take the plunge before knowing what awaits you on the other side. Like the adage goes, "Failing to plan is planning to fail", it doesn't fit any better than in this scenario, where you are trying to set up your own business. Here are some of the things that you need to look at before you set shop.

## Research

Research the chosen field thoroughly and know all there is to be familiar with, before you try it out. "Time is Money," so spend all your free time looking up the business you wish to set up. Read case studies, look out for mishaps, and check on the turnaround time to reap profits in a chosen field. Gather as much as knowledge as you can about what it is you wish to do.

Talk to friends and family about your goals, an outside perspective can be a great source to get new ideas. You may also want to consider professional advice from people who may already be doing what you wish to set up. Talk to them about the pros and cons, the kind of risks you will have to take etc. Be aware of scammers on the internet who prey on new entrepreneurs under the name of business coaches.

## Safeguard your Business Lawfully

It is of supreme importance that you register your business in accordance to the respective state laws. Negligence on this aspect may have serious implications and create redundant negative consequences for you and your business.

Typically, when you register a business, you need to notify the registrar of companies of the following happenings of your business: First, the aim and objective of your business; second, the director, the place from which you will operate and its essential memorandum, if any prepared. The names of your business associates also have to be declared. A business is not a lawfully approved until the registrar of the state authorizes it.

Get well versed with all the different business and tax regulations in your state, be thorough with laws your business is going to be governed under. There are many ambiguities in business and trade laws that can be lawfully used to your advantage to evade needless royalties and taxes. Hire a trusted legal consultant for such matters and you are good to navigate.

**Create your Unique-Selling Point**

Whatever you choose to sell or offer – your products, ideas, skills, that will generate income; they all need to be unique. There are thousands of people out there who are probably thinking about the same thing as you are. To be successful in what you do, you need to carefully plan and decide.

Chalk out a plan on how to market your idea. Think about what makes your idea stand out, who will be your target audience, why should they consider your services etc are some of the common questions you need to have concrete answers for.

You need to think ahead and have answers for these questions. While it is good to think about profit making and other nitty-gritty's as a start up business owner, always think from the customers point of view. Customer is king and customer satisfaction is the bottom-line.

Never compromise on quality, even the biggest names in the business have been reprimanded when they faltered on quality. Remember, one unsatisfied customer leads to a potential loss of future customers. Once you have clarity about the above, then you can get started with step two of your plan.

## Offer Expertise

If you aspire to set up an e-commerce site dealing with specific products, you need to have a deep understanding and knowledge about the product. For example, if your site sells homemade oils, soaps, skin care products, or Ayurvedic herbal solutions, it would be helpful if you have a degree in skin care and therapeutic studies.

This just certifies that you are an expert in the field and not someone who is selling sub-standard products that they learnt from DIY books or hear-say. Your business expertise will be solid, based on the credentials you boast of.

Testimonials help instilling confidence in consumers about your competence. Gaining consumer confidence favors you, and a satisfied customer will always recommend your services to their friends, family and extended social circle. Envision the same happening with someone who has dealt with your site. The customer base expands and you continue getting clients on a regular basis.

Ensure that your business gets you a positive assessment from your clients. The quality of your services determines your chances at growth and expansion.

# Chapter 5:
# The Common Mythical Beliefs That Must be Over Ruled

We have largely discussed about the various beliefs held by people regarding the nature of the work, which is being done from home. It is a matter of great concern that people do not take it seriously if someone is working for home. It also depends on the attitude of the incumbent that he provides the proper awareness to all the related people, so that we can jointly make a contribution towards the attainment of a better society.

Here we refer to some of the common myths which are believed by the people all around, regarding the career of working from home.

> There is a large held belief that working from home is a concern of all those people who are unable to get a job in today's competitive market. However, it is not true. All those people who are working in home with their utmost capacities are not doing this only because they have nothing to do. All these individuals have best possible potentials, but they are using these potentials in a direction different than all other people. So thinking that they are useless or they lack any kind of skill is a mere fallacy. All those who are involved in this industry must make a useful contribution breaking this fallacy.

> Another greatest fallacy, but working from home is related to the monetary benefits. The myth is related to an under paid aspect of working from home. People think that working from home is feasible only when you do not have high financial goals as they believe that it is

an underpaid sector of the job. But the reality depicts that all those who are interested in making a stable financial position can easily cherish their dreams with this unparalleled opportunity of earning money. We have to break this allay about the nature of work, working from home is as luxurious as another job. We have to break this myth and provide the utmost efforts to make this field worth working.

➢ Another myth regarding this field of working is the people's view about the lack of opportunities in working from home. You have to nullify this myth if you are also interested in this field of working. The opportunities and potentials are endless and continual. So we have to break the myth that working from home is without any further opportunities. You can generate so many possibilities and opportunities as from any other career. So apart from the feasibility generated by working from home, it generates opportunities which are surely uncountable. You can expand your way of working and you can also demonstrate these opportunities to other people enhancing their way of working. Opportunities are surely unparalleled in all areas; we just need to dig the proper potential and area which can match our particular field.

➢ Another largely held myth is the way of living adopted by the individuals who pursue working from home. People believe that working from home cannot make you entertain a good way of living. However, it is not a true fact. Many of the individuals who are pursuing their careers by working from home feel very comfortable in having such a diversified form of work which is capable of making them earn a substantive amount of financial resources. These resources are enough for them to enjoy a living which meets the standards of the society and many others living in their vicinity. So believing in the myth that working from home will not let you have a good living is totally based in fallacy. If you are resolute enough to start this career you have to put down these myths and fallacies.

If you are interested to start earning while staying at home, you undoubtedly have to break the ice and get away from these myths which can easily complicate your way towards success.

# Chapter 6:
# The Quick Fix for the Home Workers

So far we have talked about various initial thinking and thoughts about making thinking about working from home. Many people usually question the initial motivation required for starting any type of work, whether from home or by going out. In any case, you have to meet a particular standard. All we can do is to motivate ourselves that working is essential for all of us whether living in nuclear family or individual family. We have also discussed the need of the present day for making a good living and resulting urge for working.

Knowing all these realities if you have pondered upon a number of available careers, you may have also looked upon the opportunity of working from home. We ensure that if you have an inclination towards the career you have chosen a very good opportunity. We are here to motivate all those who want to make their home, their workstations, so it is the time to make our readers ready for getting into this venture, where all your work station prerequisites will be installed at your home. So we are suggesting some of the initial points which may be needed by all of you who are interested in making it a career.

**Never lose self-discipline**

If you are indulged in the career which will let you operate all your working gadgets, right in front of you in your home, you are in a better and advantageous position. You have a number of advantages which are exclusively owned only because you are a worker from home. You need not to have miles and miles of traveling. The moment you wake up you are in your office. You need not to pick up a car or any other transportation to make you reach your office. Your home being your work station provides a number of blessings. But despite of all these blessings you have to keep in mind the need for the self-discipline. Although home, being the work station consists of many benefits, yet the chances of losing the discipline are many. So before you start up with this work, make yourself resolute for being self-determined and motivated.

## Be your own boss

We have elaborated that all your work and family requirements will be fully filled at home, when you are working remotely from your home. In this scenario you have to make a proper list if things. Your mission and goals are related to your work, and your dreams and desires are pertaining to your family life. It will help you to keep both the things in balance and without any clashes. You have to perform a dual role, both as a boss as well as a worker. You have to keep yourself streamlined with your routine, just as a boss or supervisors keeps a strict eye on his workers. As there is no check over you in the home, only you are the one who can make your career a perfect success by keeping all the things within a proper format. Although supervisors are needed to make the team members work, yet the personal determination of individual members is necessary for the ultimate success. So when you are working from home you have to become your own boss.

## You have to avoid the distracting feelings

Sitting in a corporate culture or having a work station in proper office settings makes you feel like a worker, where all your attentions must be diverted towards the fulfillment of your responsibilities. Being in an office, with your boss refrain you from a number of side activities and overwhelming feelings; Sometimes the burden of work in the office makes you forget all your other responsibilities or problems. But being at home, and being in an informal setting, can make you get overburdened with your feelings. One thing that is used by workers who work from home is the abundance of distracting feelings. They feel diverted with a number of thoughts. Sometimes the work gets affected by these feelings. So if you are starting your form the home, make sure that you have devised any substantive measures for handling these kinds of feelings. You are no less than anyone; all you have to do is to keep focused and alert.

**You may indulge in over working**

If you have to work by official timings at a real time office, you will be provided with a concrete and definite job description. This job description will be decided for a definite salary and other related benefits. Every month you be entitled to all these preset monetary benefits and rewards. But when a person works from home, there are usually no preset rewards which can be confirmed. The individual picks the project and charge the amount accordingly. Most of the people when get into this work that they feel that they can earn up to limitless level. So they start picking one project after the other and in this quest they leave everything behind. Even their health and physical strength is sacrificed and they leave everything. Overworking is one of the greatest traps of working from home. If you are also having a career in this field, you have to set a deadline and a limit for your working hours, beyond which you will not be available.

**Be cautious about choice of project**

Another major concern for all the workers of this industry is the choice of a reliable client or working agency for whom they work. It is not enough to prepare yourself only to start this work; you also need to check for the credibility of the other party. If you are taking some task to do from home, you must know all the details of the work as well as the particulars of the party for whom you are working. You must clarify all the terms and conditions as well as the mode of payment that will be adopted. In case of even a slight ambiguity it is your right that you ask about the details. You need to have a full confirmation about the type of project for which you are being employed. Working for a prestigious project is always worthwhile.

## Stay attentive to market's demand:

Offer services that have a market for and buyers would be interested in. You have to put forward something that people really would like or need. If you cater to something that nobody really cares about, you'll fail at your venture sooner than you realise.

## Enjoy what you do:

It is important that you are passionate about the vocation as well. If you don't enjoy what you do, then sooner or later, it will be the same as the other jobs you had prior to starting up your own business. Discover something that interests you and something that you are good at so you don't get bored of what you do. This will keep you going to excel at what you do.

## The customer is always right:

Never leave the customers waiting. The utmost imperative aspect to success is making sure your clients are pleased. You have to give them what they want and help them out. Remember -without customers you won't have a business.

**Enjoy what you do:**

Try and be different. Don't duplicate or offer what someone else is already offering. Consumers are always looking out for different alternatives. Strive to make your product or service superior and show them why they should prefer to do business with you than others in the same business.

**It's not a weakness to get help:**

You couldn't' possibly do it all by yourself. You are going to need support and help as well. Maybe you start out alone but if you expand your business you will need people to help you with the growth you plan for your business. Hire appropriate people as you think of expanding. You can also take help from family members. Not everyone is your competition; you could instead build collaborations and strengthen your business.

**Build a plan:**

Don't get preoccupied when you start out, be pragmatic and structure your strategy and fix your thoughts. Work effectively towards making them possible. You might abruptly sense that something else sounds better or more lucrative, but you'll head nowhere if you continue drifting. There won't be any results with this kind of an approach. You need to focus on a specific niche and consistently build it.

**Patience is a virtue:**

Don't expect an instant success, you'd be fooling yourself. Sometimes people get into things in an overenthusiastic manner, but this would not work always. It takes time and effort to get success in anything you do in life. You need to invest as much as you expect. It could take quite some time to see the results you want. If you are actually passionate about it, continue working towards it and you will definitely see results.

## Have faith:

It could be really difficult in the initial stages of setting up a business and you may lose hope but just keep going. Eventually you will get where you want, if you are determined to perform and work towards it.

## Investing isn't spending:

You already know that a business can be on track with minimal investments. Nevertheless, like any other business, in due course, you need to contribute towards investments. These investments could be on different things like up-skilling yourself, improving your website, marketing etc. Wise investments like these make a difference in the returns you anticipate or want to see.

# Chapter 7:
# 10 Ways to Earn an Income from Home

Let us face the truth before you take a plunge; it may not be easy. It may be a bumpy ride, but only initially. You need to be patient, focused and determined when you choose to take this route. Slowly and steadily, things will fall in place if you stay put.

If you are a salaried professional, I wouldn't advise you to quit your job right away and take the plunge into working from home, because working from home may not give you the returns you expected in the first month itself.

Do not let this dishearten you, as I said earlier – Time is money, use all your time establishing your business and fetching clients. The money will follow once you invest yourself to research and market your product or skills.

Let us now look at 10 ways to generate some income from home. Here are some ideas that can establish you as a business owner.

## Freelance Programmer and Website Developer

Being a freelancer can be extremely beneficial and it is most certainly a dream for many designers and developers. Not only do you get to choose the job you are interested in, you also have total flexibility in terms of time. If you have the skills and are a competent programmer then there are thousands of job opportunities that are available. With so many new businesses coming up and newer changes happening technologically, people are always in need of a web programmer and developer. Market yourself well and get in touch with prospective clients who may need your services. Once you get a foothold, there is no looking back.

**Freelance Graphic Designer**

Despite the proliferation of the internet, print media is undoubtedly here to stay for the near future. Advertisements, fliers, newsletters, information sheets, magazines, letters and are just some of the categories of print media that corporate industries and small businesses need. They usually prefer to get it done from freelance designers due to the low cost involved.

Since websites and online advertising call for graphic designing services as well, even if your proficiency is only in design, put forward your work samples to potential clients, including the editorial creation, printing, etc. Businesses often line up regular freelancers for some aspects of the job they are unable to do or don't have enough time to focus on.

**Accounting and Bookkeeping Services**

Accounting assignments may include QuickBooks operation or setup, billing system creation or maintenance, receivable tracking, simple accounts payable and collections. Whatever an in house accountant handles can easily be taken over by business owners themselves or a well-informed freelancer.

To save hundreds of dollars each year over hiring a local accounting firm, business owners prefer hiring a freelancer. Many clients ask for a certified home based professional while looking for a QuickBooks Online Pro. Some clients look for a part time accountant that can guide the company. Other services you can offer are general ledger, stock controlling, payroll, and salary, manual & computerized bookkeeping, year-end closing, & tax submission etc.

## Writing and Editorial Services

If you are experienced in the field of writing and copyediting, you could easily take projects and generate income from home. If not, you might want to consider some basic training unless you are awfully good with the language and grammar then you could offer one or more of these editorial services.

Here are some of the editorial services you can offer from the comforts of your own home:

- **Copyediting**: At this stage information scrutiny is done. All grammatical, typographical and stylistic errors are caught.

- **Book Doctoring**: A book doctor offers an editorial service for manuscripts, especially written by experts, who create a manuscript as best they are able to and then turn it into publishable nature.

- **Proofreading**: This is the final destination for a "completed" writing piece. Most proofreaders make sure the copyediting changes have been aptly made and no up-to-the-minute errors are created in the course of action.

- **Indexing**: There are indexing courses available and you can also make use of the indexing software.

- **Developmental Editing**: A developmental editor works with a manuscript aiming at big-picture, things like structure and content issues.

- **Magazine Article Writing**: Magazines and newspapers are a great way to start and get your writing published before undertaking the daunting task of writing a whole book.

- **Web Page Content Provider**: Creating content for a web site is a good way to make some money writing.

- **Ghost Writing**: As a ghost writer, you get paid to essentially do all the research and write the book on behalf of someone, who takes the credit and publishes it under his name.

- **Copywriting**: Also known as business writing, usually for advertising fields, this form of writing promotes a product or a service.

- **Book Writing**: Do you have an expertise in something, like a skill, such as accounting or farming? Or something more personally, such as baking? How about writing a book about it?

## Online Tutoring

If teaching is your passion and you wish to pursue your career in the same then online tutoring helps you fulfill your dream to teach and earn. Create a tutor profile; approach the profile from a parent's perspective, ask yourself questions as a parent would while looking for a tutor −

- Is the tutor qualified?

- Is the tutor an expert in the subject knowledge I'm looking for my child?

- Is the tutor affordable?

> Does the tutor have previous training or coaching experience?

Once parents want to get in touch with you, they can do so on your page via the contact form, which then sends you an email. Many websites allow you to create a profile free and begin building your very own tutoring service business.

## Cleaning Services

This is another lucrative business since people rarely have the time to clean their homes every now and then. As a business, you can target home based cleaning or small offices and restaurants. Restaurants are always in need of daily painstaking cleaning and result in a great source of steady clients. If you would be more interested in house cleaning, you don't have to spend heaps of money on advertising or marketing because your customers will come by word of mouth. Offer complimentary packages eg: free garage cleaning with the entire house etc, to make your services sound more lucrative.

## Interior Decorator

Highlight your talents to building contractors. People purchasing new homes are usually overwhelmed with the options and possibilities of home decorating. Prepare questionnaires for each major element and room in the house. Find out how the homeowner will use the home--are there children? pets? How will each room be used? Learn about task lighting and ambient lighting and other such intricate aspects of decorating.

You need to have an eye for aesthetics and also the required qualification to undertake interior decoration tasks.

Experience, training, or licensing might be needed. Once you market yourself well and keep your clients happy by exactly understanding the kind of home they prefer to live in, you will be recommended as most interior decorators grow into their business by word of mouth.

PS: Make sure your home/office is tastefully decorated, as it is considered as the face of your business.

## Accessories and Jewelry Making

If you are creative and skilled at making accessories or jewelery, sell it online. There are different ways of getting into the jewelery business and many unusual materials with which you can work. Working with metal will possibly entail the most in the way of precise tools. However, there are many materials that you may want to work with while making jewelry-- plastic, beads, glass, fabric, threads, feathers, wood... the list is endless.

You need to research on procuring the raw material at an affordable cost, invest time in creating jewelry, or hire artisans to do it for you. Set up an online store and market your products well. You need to manage logistic support and return policies.

You could also source them from across the world in small volume and sell them at a marginal price online. You always get a much wider customer base online, and your work gains exposure all over, if it is credible. Use social media to promote your online store if you can't manage a website initially.

## Bed and Breakfast

If you live in a spacious house and do not use more than a couple of rooms, then you can sublet it. Wisely utilize what you have and create a unique experience for the guest. Create cozy spaces in the rooms and make it attractive for the visitor, take pictures and post them on social media if you do not have a website yet.

Join online groups and advertise yourself. Offer discounts to regular customers, that always helps build good relationships. Remember word of mouth is the best publicity, so ask your customers to write testimonies about their experience. A happy customer is a repeat customer. So make sure you offer the best service you possibly can.

**Day Care or Pet Sitting**

Most busy people prefer the option of their child being cared for in a home environment while they are at work. Home based child-care needs have been on the rise, as opposed to a more institutionalized setting. This means that your home based childcare business can get off and running right away. Make sure you like caring for kids or else this business may blow up in your face if you are unable to take care of the kids.

If you love spending time with pets then the best thing to do is opening a pet sitting service. You need to ensure that you are skilled and equipped to care for pets. It requires almost nothing in terms of start-up costs. However, it does call for some general credentials that will cost little or nothing to get your hands on.

Your list of credentials should most likely include personal pet ownership--if not currently, at least in the past--as well as other past or current pet-related experience, including working at an vets clinic or a pet food store, or may be some animal-related business. You will have to spend a little to bond with the pet.

# Chapter 8:
## Lay the Foundation of Your Career

Working from home is no less than an extraordinary career. In the rest of the book we have extended our efforts to make you realize that if our choice is to pursue your work from home, it is not a weak choice. Everyone has the right to pursue his career, in the way he desires. Many people think that in today's world where competition has become fierce and the labor market has become so over populated, the unemployment rate has increased to an unparalleled level. So if you are not getting the opportunity to enter into the corporate world, you should consider the option of working from home.

Now we will consider how you can establish your career in the situations when you are working from home. Establishing career means that you want to have a thorough understanding of the work, which you are doing. You have not done it just for passing time. You do it with utmost courage and struggle to let everyone know that you are following a prestigious career using all the capabilities and potentials. So establishing a career in working from home is no less than a challenge.

### Make a professional profile for yourself

When you will start working for different projects while being at home, you will realize that it is no less than working as a marketing agent for your capabilities. You have to convince others that you are best in your capabilities, and none other than you is better suited for this job. You do not have the opportunity to prove yourself in front of others through body language or gestures, as the working relations are not real time, they are virtual and remotely located. All you can do is to craft an unparalleled profile for yourself which can attract a lot of people in the industry. It is through this profile that your recruiters or agents will hire you and will give you projects. If your profile is boring, dull or unattractive you cannot get the eventual benefit of working from home.

So if you want to establish a professional profile for yourself, you need to be efficient in the knowledge of your area, so that you can craft the best possible profile for yourself.

Profile making is quite a professional task; you cannot take it for granted. All you have to do is to think of yourself as a professional. Professionals are always focused towards the attainment of professional and corporate standards. So instead of applying your personal experience, you have to mention all the professional details of your skills, to make others interested in your skills and background.

## Establish Strong Social Networks

Social networks are the basis of today's modern world. Every individual, whether belonging to corporate sector or household, is having a strong social network in one way or the other. Social networks are also necessary for all those who are working from home. If you own productive and beneficial social networks you can use it to establish your career and take it to new heights. Social networks will help you build a strong reputation among your industry and you will gain a number of unlimited projects and working opportunities. You can get a number of resources if you utilize these social networks efficiently and wisely.

If you are having some hurdle in establishing your career you can easily get benefit from these social networks. Having a prominent social network will let you have a strong position among your community. If you start interpreting your knowledge in that circle you will see the remarkable changes in your career. Having a company of the renowned people in the social community will let you cherish number of benefits which will have long-lasting effects on your career. Working from home, greatly enhances the need for these social networks, as the individuals belonging to this industry are usually linked with social media platforms.

## Start getting diverse in your skills

Another major and effective step which can help you in getting a prosperous career is to start getting diverse in your skills. During the initial phase of your career you may be unable to apply this basic technique. However, as time passes you get some experience in the field of working from home; you will come to know a number of different and wider aspects of this field. All these aspects will let you learn a number of different lessons. The basic tip is to become extraordinary in your skills, so that using these skills you can enhance your career and get higher and higher on the career ladder.

Another basic key to success is to diversify you in terms of skills. If you are at the basic level of some skills or competencies, it is your professional responsibility to enhance these skills and do not let yourself remain stagnant. All this is possible if you get an understanding about the need for this diversification. As you will gain more and more skills you will be able to cater to a number of different projects. Consequently the chances of getting renowned projects are enhanced. On the other hand, if someone is having a limited number of skills he may not get enough projects to meet his financial and professional goals. So it is highly advised that once you choose working from home as your career, you have to build the professional potentials for it.

Having talked a lot about the major aspects, I think that we have made it quite clear to our readers how they can make their way towards established careers. Working from home is no less than a career so you have to make all the efforts to make it recognizable.

# Conclusion

Working from home is a blessing in disguise for many people and I am often the subject of envy for a lot of people who still juggle between home and work. Working from home requires as much as professionalism as it requires while reporting to a supervisor.

Time and flexibility are luxuries one can afford while working from home, but discipline and time management should not be neglected. Plan your day ahead the previous night and follow it through. Never do something later that you could do now. Working from home has not only offered me financial freedom, I now have the luxury of spending quality family time with my girls too.

I hope this book proves to be helpful to all those who have dreamed of earning money from home. I want to thank you once again for downloading this eBook and hope you enjoyed reading it.

*You don't have to be great to start, but you have to start to be great* - Zig Ziglar

Finally, if you enjoyed this book, please take the time to share your thoughts and post a review on Amazon. It'd be greatly appreciated!

Thank you and good luck!

www.ingramcontent.com/pod-product-compliance
Lightning Source LLC
Chambersburg PA
CBHW071017180526
45168CB00003B/1456